# Employed By Graduation

## By Kolby Goodman

For Allison, Everett, and Graham

# Contents

Don't forget to download all the additional resources for this book.

Head to:

https://www.employedbygraduation.com/

Or scan the QR Code below:

# Intro

When I graduated from college, I was full of conflicting emotions:

- Excited to finally be done!
- Relieved there were no more late nights study sessions.
- Sad to be missing friends who were still going to class.
- Anxious to see what the next months had in store for me.
- Afraid I would have to move back in with my parents.
- Hopeless because I didn't know how to get out there and find meaningful employment.
- Scared of not finding any job!
- Confused on what the right and wrong actions would be.

Don't get me wrong, adulthood is an amazing experience. Your 20's are a great time to discover who you really are as an independent human being and young professional. But those months leading up to and following college graduation were some of the most stomach-turning and stress-inducing of my life.

I made a lot of mistakes, A LOT. But after much trial and error, I was able to find a stable job with a great team that allowed me to start fully adulting, enjoy going out with my friends and traveling the world, and start my post-grad life off with a meaningful position that contributed with my short- and long-term career and personal goals.

I wish someone had handed me an organized collection of actions—not theories, not wishes, or dreams, or hopes—but concrete ACTIONS, when I walked across the stage at San Diego State University. Heck, I wish someone had given me that list of actions the moment I graduated from high school.

The life and career lessons, failures, and, ultimately, successes I went through are what compelled me to write this book. To give you—the bright, intelligent, passionate, and driven young professional—the tools necessary to go out there and show the world your value and worth. To get in front of the right people who you inspire, and who in turn inspire you, on a daily basis. To start this next exciting chapter improving your life and the lives of others. And to avoid meaningless, menial jobs that don't motivate you, stall your progress, and kill your soul.

The biggest lesson I learned in my 20's is that life is propelled forward not by a few large, monumental events, but by many small habitual ones. In order to see real change and progress in yourself, you need to take action every day.

**_This book was written so you can simply flip to a page on any given day and be driven to take that one action._**

That's it. One day, one action.

I hope you move forward through this book comforted by the actions you may already be taking, driven to execute those actions you know you should be doing more often, and confident in succeeding in this next amazing and exciting chapter in your life.

_—Kolby Goodman, Career Coach and Owner of TheJobHuntr.com_

# Plan to do one action in this book, tomorrow.

*"The best preparation for good work tomorrow is to do good work today."*
*—Elbert Hubbard, American Writer*

This year, over 1.98 million (that's million with an M!) new college graduates will enter the full-time workforce, and a large majority of them will wait until crossing the stage to start their transition into career professionals.

This staggering number, in addition to the 41% of college graduates under the age of 27[1] who are in jobs that didn't even require a 4-year degree, are your main sources of competition.

You simply cannot afford to wait. Starting your employment journey now will allow you to avoid the post-grad labor market flood that happens every summer, and beat your competition to the punch. Every action in this book is designed to give you tangible results that help get you to the ultimate goal of landing your first amazing job.

---

[1] Redden, Elizabeth, "41% of Recent Grads Work in Jobs Not Requiring a Degree," *Inside Higher Ed*, February 18th, 2020, https://www.insidehighered.com/quicktakes/2020/02/18/41-recent-grads-work-jobs-not-requiring-degree.

The key here is to take actions early and often, because
your success in this process (and every process you
encounter for the rest of your adult life) will be built
not on bursts of massive progress, but on the constant,
small execution of good actions.

Start small. Complete one action in this book today.
Then next week, do another.
Later next week, complete a third action.

Building up good momentum and continuing to move
forward will help you snowball all of your hard work to
get that first job in your career field!

Make a small commitment to yourself and your future
career today: fill out the following to help get started:

Today,                          (MM/DD/YY),
I will download and review the additional resources
from EmployeedbyGraduation.com

Next Tuesday,                          (MM/DD/YY),
I will do action #1

Next Friday,                          (MM/DD/YY),
I will do action #2.

# Section 1: Self-Discovery and Growth

# Action #1: Develop your "Why" statement

It has been scientifically proven that an employee is happier, more productive, and has higher long-term success if they are able to apply their personal passions to their professional pursuits. Now more than ever, companies are looking for ways to maximize on-the-job results by actively integrating these passionate professionals into their teams.

You need to, without a shadow of a doubt, know what your personal passions are and identify the "Why" of the career you have chosen for yourself.

Ask yourself these questions to best pinpoint your "Why":

1)      What am I really good at?
2)      What do other people tell me I am good at?
3)      What problems do I like solving?
4)      How do I make the world a better place?
5)      How do I *want* to make the world a better place?

Answering these questions will help you start down the path of fully fleshing out your "Why" statement.

My "Why" statement looks like this:

*I live to teach and empower human beings to better themselves, contribute more to the world, and increase their earning potential through enhancing their careers.*

Your "Why" statement can act as a thesis for your job candidacy—a statement you can reflect back on when you are unclear of who you are and what value you can bring as a professional.

Type it up. Print it out. Tape it to your bathroom mirror. The more you remind yourself of your "Why", the more focused you will be on the actions you take from here on out.

Write your "Why" statement below:

# Action #2: Identify the problems you can solve

A large majority of candidates, both young and old, start the application process by asking the question, "Why am I qualified?" On the other hand, hiring managers start looking at candidates by asking, "How can this person help solve our problems?"

Set yourself apart from other young professionals by knowing exactly how your experience, education, and passions can solve the problems of the companies you want to work for.

Think about a job you just applied for or are going to apply for next. Below you will find a series of questions that will help you start to identify the problems you can solve in that job or company:

***Printable Worksheet available in Downloadable Resources***

*The Company:*
What problems is the company solving?
What is their mission?
Their vision?
Who are their biggest, best, favorite customers?

*The Job:*
What problems is the company looking for the person in the job to solve?
What short-term problems?
What long-term problems?
What everyday problems?

*You:*
What problems can you solve?
What problems have you successfully solved in the past?
What problems do you think you can solve in the future?
Why do you feel equipped to solve those problems?

*The Big Picture:*
What problems can I help my next company solve?
Why am I qualified to solve these problems?
What are the positive outcomes of solving these problems?

Now, when you  go into your next interview, start your next application, or have your next professional conversation, you can have the answers to the above questions in mind. You will automatically give yourself value, be what managers are looking for, and set yourself apart from the rest of the pack.

Today,                              (MM/DD/YY),
I got a clearer understanding of the problems I can help my next employer solve.

---

# Action #3: Record your biggest professional accomplishments

*"What you are will show in what you do."*
—*Thomas Edison*

While many new professionals clog their resumes and overwhelm their interviews with all the job responsibilities they had in the past, those individuals completely misunderstand how employers value candidates: Results.

Ultimately, managers will base your potential not simply on IF you can do the job, but HOW WELL you can do it. And the most powerful way to show them how well you can do the job? By presenting concrete evidence of past professional accomplishments, wins, and successes. When you do this, potential employers are given a much better understanding of your on-the-job performance and, as a result, start to picture you bringing similar success to their company.

Write down your top 2 professional accomplishments along with  related information to help your next employer understand what you are capable of:

****Printable Worksheet available in Downloadable Resources****

My #1 professional accomplishment is:

It is #1 because:

The 3 actions I took to accomplish this goal were:

The biggest obstacle I had to overcome to accomplish this goal was:

My #2 professional accomplishment is:

It is #2 because:

The 3 actions I took to accomplish this goal were:

The biggest obstacle I had to overcome to accomplish this goal was:

Today, ___________________ (MM/DD/YY), I wrote down my 2 biggest professional accomplishments and have 2 great stories to tell in my next interview.

# Action #4: Create your ideal job characteristics list

Going for "any job available" is not the ideal or most effective way to kickstart the hunt for your first career job. Trying to be everything to everybody will ensure you become nothing to no one.

You need to niche-down and have a very clear picture of your ideal job so you can better market yourself and target those opportunities. As author Zig Ziglar once said, "If you aim at nothing, you will hit it every time."

Here are some important job characteristics you need to identify to give yourself a better understanding of your ideal position. These are based on the popular Job Characteristics Theory (JTF), developed in the mid 1970's by Greg R. Oldham and J. Richard Hackman, business professors at the University of Illinois and Harvard, respectively[2].

---

2  Lumen, "Job Design and Job Characteristics Theory," https://courses.lumenlearning.com/wm-introductiontobusiness/chapter/job-design-and-job-characteristics-theory/

- *Skill Variety*: To what degree does your ideal job incorporate various activities? The more variety in your daily actions, the more meaning you may be able to get from the job.
- *Task Identity*: Do the results of your actions have a visible outcome? Tangible results help employees better understand their contribution and become more engaged in their job duties.
- *Task Significance*: Is what you are doing on the job having a positive effect on the lives of others? This can either be with the company itself or with external stakeholders. You feel more meaning from a job that substantially improves the well-being of others than a job that has a limited effect on anyone else.
- *Autonomy*: How much freedom, independence, and discretion are you given by management to plan out and execute your work? Do you want this autonomy? How much direction and oversight do you need to be truly successful?
- *Feedback*: How would you like to receive feedback on your results? How clear, specific, detailed, and *actionable* is the information you are receiving about the effectiveness of your job performance? You are not always going to be perfect, so making sure there is a sound structure for productive feedback could be key to helping you exceed future job expectations.

****Printable Worksheet available in Downloadable Resources****

Go through each of the 5 sections above and choose 1 question within each section to answer.

- *Skill Variety*
- *Task Identity*
- *Task Significance:*
- *Autonomy:*
- *Feedback:*

# Action #5: Create your ideal employer bucket list

An important step to landing your ideal first career job is to identify where you are going to start said job. Company culture is second to compensation when it comes to the characteristics professionals find most important when starting off their career.

On top of having the technical skills to succeed on the job, companies—now more than ever—are looking for candidates who are a "good fit" for the team. Identifying your ideal company culture can help ensure long-term success in your career, while at the same time prepping you to become an ideal candidate for those companies.

If you are clear on what you are looking for in your next employer, you can actively pursue those characteristics and continuously demonstrate how you can do a great job while melding well with their culture.

Below are some identifying categories your next company will have. Go through each category and select or write down the things you most want out of each:

****Printable Worksheet available in Downloadable Resources****

---

*Company Size:* I want to work at a
small  medium   large company (circle one)


*Industry*
I want to work in one of these 3 industries:

1)

2)

3)


*Company Values and Mission*
I want my next company to have the following values
for itself and their employees:

1)

2)

3)

I want my next company's mission to be focused on:


*Community Engagement*
I want my next company to positively contribute to the
community by:

*Rewards and Recognition*
I want my next company to reward and recognize their employees by:



*Work/Life Balance*
I want my next company to encourage a balance between work and life by:

# Action #6: Know what salary to expect

In order to ensure you are receiving fair compensation at your next job, you need to know what the market rate is for a new professional like yourself.

Factors like education, length and type of professional experience, industry, job title, and geographic location all contribute to your final annual salary. There are some great tools out there to help you determine this figure, and having this information handy when you go in for an interview is important.

Knowing what salary to expect  gives you leverage, makes you aware of what you're worth, and can help you understand what may be able to garner you a higher take-home wage.

Here are some salary calculators you can use to see a range of how much you should expect to be paid:

PayScale.com - $                          /year
Salary.com – $                            /year
SalaryExpert.com - $                      /year
Indeed.com/Salary $                       /year


According to the above sources, I should  expect to earn about
$                                         in my first year.

# Action #7: Understand the types of professionals who can help you find a job

Internal recruiters, external recruiters, headhunters, and career coaches may prove to be very important for helping you transition from college to career. Understanding how each of these professionals works and how you can best utilize them will give you that extra advantage.

**Internal Recruiter**: employed full-time by the hiring company. Dedicated resource to source, select, and pre-screen high-quality candidates for internal job opportunities. These people typically do not work on commission and are paid on a full-time basis by their companies.

**External Recruiter / Headhunter**: contracted on a per-position basis by the hiring company. Works for a dedicated placement or recruiting firm. Outsourced professional responsible for sourcing, selecting, and pre-screening high-quality candidates for hiring company job opportunities. Performs light interview coaching. Typically works on commission through the recruiting firms. Opportunities are typically classified as permanent, contract-to-hire, or contract.

**Reverse Recruiter**: contracted by the professional to source and screen high-quality opportunities. Performs interview coaching and edits professional documents. Typical clients are tenured professionals and executives garnering over six figures per year. Typically works on commission or service-fee basis paid for by the candidate.

**Career Coach**: contracted by a professional to assist with preparation for job search, professional documents, and interviews. Clients range from new college graduates to professionals looking for a new job or career. These professionals help provide the tools and guidance needed for a focused and successful job search. Typically works on a service-fee basis.

Today _______________ (MM/DD/YY), I learned more about how these 4 different professionals can help me in my job search.

# Section 2: Professional Relationship Building

# Action #8: Cultivate your network today

With practically everyone carrying around a tiny, internet-connected computer in their pocket, communication is now at an all-time high. But you could also argue that the quality of this communication is not as meaningful as it used to be.

In an instant you can message a friend in another state, send a photo to your grandma, or have a video conversation with someone on the other side of the globe. And as amazing as these leaps in technology are, don't allow them to completely replace your efforts at interacting face-to-face.

In the next 7 days, take an interaction that you would have normally done by email, text, or social media, and transform it into a more personal interaction.

Set up a face-to-face conversation with a digital-first friend for casual 30-minute chat. You two can catch up on life, see how classes are going, or ask them about their own job search.

The goal is to get you comfortable with engaging in a more personal and rapport-building manner when it is normally all too easy to punch out a few messages or send a meme digitally.

Person I will contact:


Normal method of contact:
Phone/Email/Text/Social Media (circle one)

Date and time of meeting:

# Action #9: Attend a meeting of an organization on campus

Student orgs are amazing ways to get connected to your campus, meet new people, and hone your leadership skills. While attending San Diego State University, I got involved in an amazing organization called Alpha Kappa Psi where I was able to learn more about myself as a young professional and really blossom as a leader and teacher. I met my best friends—heck, even my future wife—while involved in AKPsi, and still treasure and utilize those relationships today.

Even though I found one great organization to be part of, I wish I would have joined additional organizations on campus to broaden my horizons and expand my network.

Joining multiple organizations allows you to experience different leadership styles, interact with young professionals who have diverse personal and career interests, and gives you additional opportunities to lead.

Right now, go to your school's website and find the list of active student orgs currently on your campus. Pick 2 that interest you, note the times and dates of their next meeting, and note the email address of the president or point of contact for the organization:

1) Name:

Date:

Point of contact email:

2) Name:

Date:

Point of contact email:

Now, email the point of contact for that organization to introduce yourself, letting them know you are planning to attend their next meeting.

This quick email will ensure that you don't end up feeling alone in the sea of other attendees, plus it gets you in contact with the leader of the org.

Make sure to seek out the president and/or the person you were emailing with at the meeting you attend and formally introduce yourself. This will be your first contact at this new organization.

---

# Action #10: Attain a leadership position in a student group

*"Leadership does take work. And it should. If you aspire to be a leader, you ought to treat leadership as a craft, you ought to become a student of it, and you ought to work at it. And if you're not willing to work at it, well, you get what you give."*
—*Douglas Conant, CEO of Campbell Soup Company*

If all you're doing is attending meetings and paying dues, you're not getting as much out of your student organizations as you could be. Gaining a leadership or executive board role can provide you with priceless opportunities to lead, manage projects, and sharpen your public speaking skills.

You don't necessarily have to be the president or vice-president of an organization, either. Find where your passions or skills lie and figure out how they can be used to help improve your student organization in a leadership position.

Challenging yourself now, while the stakes are low, allows you to make mistakes and learn in a low-risk environment. It also gives you some amazing experience to put on your resume and show your next employer your successful abilities as a leader or manager.

Fill in the blanks below to help start your path to a leadership position:

Organization I want to help lead:


Title of position I want:


Name of person currently holding position:

(Schedule a meeting with them to learn more about the position)

Date of next elections:

# Action #11: Schedule a time to chat one-on-one with your favorite professor

Your professors have been in their industry or at your school for a very long time. They've seen a lot of similar students come their way, and they've probably helped a lot of those past students get their careers started as well. Utilizing this resource could be a welcome shortcut on your journey to landing that first career job.

Before you set up a meeting (or pop in during office hours), make sure you structure the conversation to maximize everyone's time. Come prepared with direct questions to ask your professor, and make sure you get the answers you are looking for.

Below are 5 sample questions you could ask:

1) What is the #1 mistake you see former students making when looking for a job after graduation?
2) How have you seen students apply what they've learned or done in the classroom to their careers?
3) What are the top traits employers are looking for in candidates with my education?

4) If I am looking to be a
   (position/title you want 10 years from now),  what
   kind of jobs should I be looking for now?
5) What are the top 3 companies in your field that you
   feel are a great place for a new graduate like myself
   to start my career?
 Now that you have an idea of the kinds of questions
you should be asking, take 5 minutes right now and
come up with 5 of your own questions:

6)
7)
8)
9)
10)

Great!


Don't monopolize the time of your busy professors. Out
of the 10 questions above, pick the top 4 you would
most like to have answered. Those will be the 4
questions you prepare for the meeting.

Make sure to take notes during your conversation and
ask clarifying questions to get more detailed
information. This valuable information has the ability to
give you an edge over your professional competition.

I have scheduled a meeting with Prof.              (name)
on                    (MM/DD/YY).

___

My questions and their responses:

1q)
1a)



2q)
2a)



3q)
3a)



4q)
4a)

# Action #12: Have one sit-down conversation with a professional

While you may hear this advice given freely to many active job seekers, don't go out there and conduct "Informational Interviews." These kinds of meetings are all too often one-sided, single-dimensional interactions that don't really get you anywhere. Instead, go and have a "Professional Conversation."

So, what is the difference between the two?

A Professional Conversation serves to help you connect and build rapport with another professional. Additionally, these types of conversations help you gather specific information, introduce you to other professionals, and could even give you a job opportunity.

Similar to Action #11, your homework here will consist of preparing questions that will help you better understand what is needed to succeed both as a new graduate looking for a job and as a new professional with lofty career aspirations.

Set up a meeting with a professional you already know;
don't worry if this professional isn't in a career field
related to what you want to do. Your goal is to learn
more about their career journey: their education, how
they got their first job out of college, and why they're
doing what they're doing today.

These conversations are great if you are still trying to
figure out what you want to do with your career, but
they also help you better understand the steps needed
to be successful no matter what career path you
choose.

If you are able, offer to pay for the professional's lunch
or coffee. It's the least you can do for taking up their
valuable time.

Today, I contacted                    (name of professional)
by email / phone/ in person /Zoom to have (lunch/
coffee) on                            (MM/DD/YY).

My questions and their responses

1q)
1a)

2q)
2a)


3q)
3a)


4q)
4a)

# Action #13: Find a mentor

*"I've seen that phenomenally successful people believe they can learn something from everybody. I call them 'mavericks with mentors.'"*
*—Brendon Burchard, New York Times bestselling author*

A large majority of successful people have actively sought the counsel and advice of someone older, wiser, and with more professional and life experience. These successful people know the value of perspective, knowledge, and mentorship. In order to truly take your career to the heights you want, I highly recommend getting a mentor in your life.

At the end of a particularly positive and engaging Professional Conversation (from Action #12), follow up one day later via email. Thank the professional for his or her time and close with a strong "call to action"— asking if the professional would be open to having similar conversations with you on a regular basis.

Your follow up may look something like this:

*"Thank you again for meeting with me. I know you are very busy, and I appreciate you taking the time to help me start my journey. You provided me with so much value and inspiration and I now have a better understanding of the work ahead of me.*

*I would love to continue our relationship and was wondering if we could meet up again next month so I can catch you up on my progress. How does Tuesday the 7th at 4pm work for you?"*

I would recommend <u>against</u> using the term "mentor" in this email. Since the structure and boundaries of your relationship aren't set quite yet, throwing out a title as heavy as "mentor" could scare away a valuable resource and end a great professional relationship.

This person should be looked at like your primary care doctor: a professional you see on a semi-regular basis with the goal of preventative (or proactive) action. Do not treat this professional like a 9-1-1 call or the emergency room for your future career.

I have reached out to the following professionals for ongoing conversations:

1)

2)

3)

# Action #14: Attend your first professional organization meeting

There are countless local, national, and international professional organizations designed to help you deepen your industry knowledge, build your network, and add to your professional experience. As a young professional, getting engaged with these organizations now will help you even more than if you wait until you're "established" in your career.

Head over to Google and search:

"(Industry) organization (Your City)"

As you do your research, here are a few things to take note of:

1) How many chapters does this org have?
2) Are the events mainly social/networking, educational, or a mix of both?
3) Who is on the board/leadership committee of this org?

Write down the 3 organizations that interest you the most. Also note when each of them will be having their next live (or virtual) event:

1)
Date:
2)
Date:

3)
Date:

Now, I want you to commit to attending one of the
above events:

I will attend the                                    (event)
on                            (MM/DD/YY).

Your first professional organization meeting will be
scary, and that is okay. The goal is to get this first event
done and to go on to the next one feeling more
comfortable and engaged. Getting involved in a
professional organization at such an early point in your
career can help you move forward from position to
position and company to company.

# Action #15: Reconnect with a professional from your past

Now that you are making it a priority to actively expand your network, you need to make sure those relationships don't die on the vine. Many new professionals are good at quickly snapping up email addresses or phone numbers at professional events, but you need to separate yourself from the Average Joe college student looking for a job by making sure you turn these one-time interactions into long-term professional relationships.

Pick one professional from your past—an old boss, former teacher, friend's parent—and directly reach out to that professional to schedule a meeting.

Get in the habit of reconnecting and meeting with these acquaintances on a more regular basis.

The more often you reconnect and meet up, the deeper those relationships will become and the more these professionals from your past will be able to help you as you pursue your first post-college job.

These are also great people to ask to be your professional references moving forward.

Name of professional from your past:

___

Method of contact:  Email / Phone / Other  (circle one)

Date of contact:

Date of meeting:

# Action #16: Talk to one professional who has done it already

*"Education is what remains after one has forgotten what one has learned in school."*
*—Albert Einstein*

One of the best ways to avoid costly and time-consuming missteps when starting out in your career is by learning from the mistakes of others. And the best way to learn about those mistakes (and shoehorn in some professional networking as well) is by going directly to the source.

Take a look at your social, professional, or alumni network and find a career professional in the industry or role you are aiming for, who has 10 years or less experience, and who has successfully made the transition from college to career. Utilize the power of the LinkedIn search to help you pinpoint these professionals.

Set up a quick meeting and come prepared with questions geared towards learning more about this professional's journey from college graduation to where they are now in their career.

Find out what they did right, the things they attribute to "luck," and what they would not do again.

As you learn from someone else's life lessons, this also allows you to get a bit personal and build some rapport. Setting the stage to start a genuine, long-term professional relationship.

Name of professional:

Current job title:

College major:

Date contacted:

Meeting date:

Top 3 takeaways from your meeting:

1)


2)


3)

Don't forget to download all the additional resources for this book.

Head to:

**https://www.employedbygraduation.com/**

Or scan the QR Code below:

# Action #17: Connect with 3 new professionals

It's really easy to get comfortable in our own social circles. There is none of the dreaded awkwardness, you already hang out with these people on a regular basis, and that built- in history makes it easier to connect and bond. But in order to successfully and quickly make the transition from student to career professional, you need to actively be going out into the world and meeting new, professional adults.

The best part is that many career professionals love helping out eager and determined new graduates like you. They see it as an opportunity to give back and positively contribute to the start of a new career. And they may have gotten similar help back when they first started, so paying it forward is a natural action.

There are plenty of opportunities to connect with professionals, but here are my 2 favorites:

1) **Ask for introductions from professionals you already know.** Ask a professional already in your network if they could introduce you to someone they know. Specify what type of industry or job title you are looking to connect with. Mention that you would like to ask a few questions that should only take 20 minutes of their time.

2) **Contact guest speakers or lecturers.** Next time you have a guest in a class or student org meeting, make it a priority to message or go up to them after their talk and introduce yourself. Let them know what you liked about their presentation and ask if you could learn more about one aspect of their expertise over a quick meeting or call.

In the next 10 days, set up meetings with 3 new professionals. Make it a point to have an engaging and interactive conversation.

Professional #1:

Date of meeting:

Professional #2:

Date of meeting:

Professional #3:

Date of meeting:

# Action #18: Add unexpected value to one other professional

*"Life's most persistent and urgent question is, 'What are you doing for others?'"*
*—Martin Luther King Jr.*

In the transition from college to career, it's really easy to take and take and take—from getting introductions and gathering information to taking up valuable time and outright asking for jobs. If you are not careful, you may start being seen as a taker, or worse: a stereotypically selfish young professional.

To combat this attitude, you need to actively and positively contribute to the lives of other professionals. Proactively show your network how you can be a valuable part of it, and not just a continuous leech.

You may not feel like you have a lot to contribute to others, but that assumption is far from the truth.

Your personal story and journey may help inspire or guide others.
You may be an expert in a subject that could help someone else.

Or you may know two people who could greatly benefit from an introduction to one another.

A very simple and easy way to add value to others is by sharing interesting information that relates to them professionally, _or personally_, and isn't just another funny video or meme.

Next time you are online and you see a unique article/video/piece of content, share it with someone who may be interested. Send the link over email and briefly explain why you wanted to share it with them.

Here is an example:

_"Hey Anne,_

_I found this awesome article over on Forbes.com that talks about the major hurdles professionals under 35 are facing when it comes to retirement planning._

_Since this is the target demographic for your new venture, I wanted to pass it along!_

_(LINK)"_

_Or_

*"Hey David,*

*I remembered you mentioned an upcoming trip to Alaska at our last networking event. And that you were bringing all of your camera gear.*

*Stumbled across this cool video related to wildlife photography in Alaska and wanted to pass it along.*

*Hope you enjoy!*

*(LINK)"*

The goal with these "random acts of value" is to quickly and easily help others, and cultivate a genuine and reciprocal relationship.

Today                                    MM/DD/YY),
I sent
a link about

---

# Action #19: Send a thank you card

*"Develop an attitude of gratitude, and give thanks for everything that happens to you, knowing that every step forward is a step toward achieving something bigger and better than your current situation."*
*—Brian Tracy, Motivational Public Speaker and Self-Development Author*

While we may say it often, actually showing appreciation seems to be a lot less prevalent in our day-to-day lives.

I want you to take action and send a thank you card to someone who has positively influenced you. Their actions don't have to be life-changing or overly monumental, even something as simple as a ride to the airport or cooking you dinner is enough to warrant your gratitude.

This simple act of sitting down, writing out (by hand!), and dropping a physical card in the mail can really make someone's day and remind them why you value their relationship.

While you should be sending similar messages after every one of your professional interviews, getting in the habit of sending "just because" thank you cards will encourage your network to want to help you more, and remind you of why you should be grateful even when you don't feel like you have a lot to be grateful for.

Today ________________________ (MM/DD/YY), I wrote a thank you note to ________________ (name) about ________________ (their nice thing).

# Section 3: Marketing Yourself on the Page and Screen

# Action #20: Update your resume to sell you based on benefits, not just features

During high school and college, we tend to have jobs that are mainly based in service and labor: flipping pizzas, delivering newspapers, waiting tables, etc. In turn, the way we write our resumes tends to reflect on the menial, mind-numbing tasks we were doing in those kinds of jobs. Our early resumes are very basic, simply listing out our duties and responsibilities.

And while that is fine if you are going for another hourly wage job, this will not cut it as you pursue your first career position. Your next employer does need to know your skills and expertise, but if that is all you are selling yourself on, you are leaving out valuable information.

Expand your resume by tying your tasks and responsibilities to the positive outcomes and impacts you have been able to create. Why is what you do on a day-to-day basis at your job important? Who does it help? How does it help them? How is what you are doing on the job save time, reduce costs, or increase profit?

These questions need to be answered on your resume because they are the exact ones the hiring manager is looking for!

Here is an example before and after of a resume bullet that has now incorporated the individual's benefits:

Before: *Utilize Facebook advertising and Google AdWords to lead sales*

After: *Lead paid Facebook and Google advertising, develop ad copy and graphics, create online forms to gather information, and actively monitor impression, click through, and cost per click metrics and adjust audience and copy to improve engagement; ads directly resulted in an additional $80,000 in revenue.*

Now it's your turn!

One bullet on my resume that needs to be improved is:

Here is my improved bullet:

# Action #21: Remove cliché buzzwords and phrases

An easy red flag that indicates a professional has no clue what their value is and what their skill sets are is an overuse of buzzwords on their professional documents.

These buzzwords are easily identifiable by any hiring manager because they sound good, but ultimately they give no true indication of what kind of professional value a candidate can bring to the role. Buzzwords don't illustrate measurable characteristics, they're not backed up by facts or figures, and they're ultimately overused in the course of the document.

Here are 10 of the most overused buzzwords seen on resumes today:

- Motivated
- Creative
- Passionate
- Driven
- Extensive experience
- Organizational
- Strategic
- Track record
- Responsible
- Problem-solving

Notice how these words, when seen on top of one another, start to lose all meaning? Let's make sure your resume is not like that!

These buzzwords appear on my current resume      ## times.


Today                         (MM/DD/YY), I replaced them with words that are more impactful and unique.

# Action #22: Stop using your .edu email address

You're on the path to being a full-fledged professional adult! So now is the exact right time to stop acting like a regular college kid and quit using your .edu address.

When an employer spots an .edu address on a resume or application, they assume you are still in school—not yet able or ready to commit to a full-time job—and will most likely put you in the "no" pile.

Make sure you're giving the right first impression by using a professionally tailored, non-.edu, email address:

*FirstNameLastName at email dot com*

Google's Gmail is your best bet for your new professional email. You should also stop using your .edu address so that you don't lose out on any future opportunities. If you apply to a job now, even though you may not qualify, you will stay in that company's candidate database forever. So in the future, long after you have forgotten the password to your .edu email or the school has shut it down, that employer may reach out and you will end up missing a great opportunity.

I have updated my email address on:
- ☐ Resume
- ☐ Cover Letter
- ☐ LinkedIn
- ☐ Job Board Sites

# Action #23: Optimize your resume for applicant-tracking systems

Did you know that before your next application is even seen by a human eye, it will be painstakingly picked over by the company's applicant-tracking systems? ATS, for short, is a dedicated piece of software that sorts, reviews, and approves applications for job openings. Your application will be processed through this automated computer system designed to pick out high-quality candidates based on a set of very cut-and-dried criteria, like years of experience and specific keywords.

In order to get in the good graces of this computer system and move on to the company's recruiter, HR coordinator, or hiring manager, you need to make sure you're showing the computer what it wants to see. The most direct way to do this is by identifying and utilizing the 10 most common phrases and keywords from the job posting itself in your application and resume. This will allow you to speak directly to your ATS audience using its exact language.

There are many phrase counters and resume analysis sites online, and you can go download the resources to get a list of them.

Start by uploading your resume and the job you are interested in and write down the following:

The top 10 phrases on my job postings are:

1)

2)

3)

4)

5)

6)

7)

8)

9)

10)

My current resume has a _______% match rate.

# Action #24: Update your LinkedIn profile

Over the last 10 years, a LinkedIn profile has evolved from being a nice-to-have to a need-to-have when it comes to applying for professional positions.

Why? Because 87% of all hiring managers and recruiters are using LinkedIn to research and source qualified job candidates[3]. And only 12%(!) of professionals between the ages of 20 and 35 are active on the site.

If you haven't already, go to LinkedIn.com and sign up for an account. Or if you are like a large majority of young professionals, log back into the site for the first time in a long time and take a look around.

The 3 things you should immediately do to update your profile:

1)  Update your professional profile picture

2)  Update your contact info to a personal email (no .edu accounts!)

---

[3] Jobvite, *Jobvite Recruiter Nation Reports,* https://www.jobvite.com/blog/what-every-job-seeker-should-know-jobvites-2020-recruiter-nation-survey

3)  Add 10 professionals that you already know as
    LinkedIn connections

Spend 15 minutes exploring the site. Look at your news
feed, check your messages, and accept any pending
connection requests.

The quicker you can integrate LinkedIn into your career
search routine, the more value you will get out of it.

# Action #25: Optimize your LinkedIn Headline

As you update your LinkedIn profile, you'll find that a lot of the default settings on your profile aren't the best for a young professional looking to start their career.

For example, LinkedIn automatically defaults your Headline, the 140-character field located right below your name, to your most recent job title and employer. But since you aren't looking for the job you already have, update this right away.

Key items to list in your Headline include:

- **Desired next job titles**: Marketing Coordinator, Jr. Engineer, Hotel Sales Associate, etc.

- **Important job-related skill sets**: Project Coordination, Drafting, Contract Management, etc.

- **Prominent industry-specific technologies:** Hootsuite, AutoCAD, Opera CRM, etc.

Here is a version of my LinkedIn Headline:

Career Coach | Keynote Speaker | Resume Editor | Interview | LinkedIn | Professional Networking

Your updated Headline will help your profile appear higher in the LinkedIn search results and be noticed by recruiters and hiring managers.

My new LinkedIn Headline is:

# Action #26: Ask for 3 LinkedIn Recommendations

What if there was a way for your next employer to learn what your professional references have to say about you and your work without having to pick up the phone? You're in luck because there is, and it's called a LinkedIn Recommendation.

LinkedIn Recommendations are a great way to provide "social proof" to your next employer. These testimonials about your past work from bosses, co-workers, or professors positively add to your candidacy by providing personal stories about the quality and professionalism that you've brought to previous jobs, volunteer opportunities, leadership positions, or the classroom.

Think of LinkedIn Recommendations  like Yelp reviews for your career: the more you have, the more opportunities you will have, and the better chance you give yourself to get in the good graces of your future employer.

Start pursuing Recommendations from career adults, not from fellow college students. Here is a sample message you can send, within LinkedIn, to ask for your next Recommendation:

*"Hi Randy,*

*Hope all is well!*

*I am starting to ramp up the search for my first career job after college, and I'm incorporating LinkedIn heavily.*

*I know LinkedIn Recommendations can help my next employer better understand the kind of work I am capable of, and I would love for you to share your experience working with me on the digital marketing strategy modernization project and how we launched the new website.*

*The Recommendation only needs to be 3-5 sentences long, and should take you all of 2 minutes.*

*Thanks in advance for your help on this! I really appreciate it!"*

Send 3 LinkedIn Recommendation requests to 3 different professionals within the next day. And make a regular habit of reaching out and asking for more Recommendations for your next job.

Professional 1)

Professional 2)

Professional 3)

—

# Action #27: Include a cover letter with every application

Unlike in the past, not all job applications today require a cover letter. And since that's the case, many job candidates assume that it is totally unnecessary to write one and will not submit a cover letter. But since you're reading this book, I have to assume you were never one to just do the bare minimum.

Set yourself apart from the rest of the applicants by including a cover letter with every single application you submit. Your job is to give the employer as much relevant information on your experience as possible, and this letter will give them a greater understanding of you as a professional and help them determine if you're qualified and a good fit for the position.

Withholding information, especially the kind of information you can provide in a cover letter, is detrimental to your job candidacy and may ultimately cost you amazing future opportunities.

As a chief marketing officer of a leading retail franchise once told me, "I look for tie breakers when I hire, it helps me separate similarly qualified candidates. And a cover letter is a very easy and direct way to break a tie."

If you have already applied to a bunch of positions, go back and see if it's possible to supplement your application with an updated cover letter. You can either add it to the set of documents you already uploaded, or email it over to the HR rep or hiring manager.

Last 3 jobs I applied to:

| Job Title | Company | CL Y/N? |
| --- | --- | --- |
|  |  |  |
|  |  |  |
|  |  |  |

# Action #28: Now, write a cover letter that is better than all the others

Now that you are including a cover letter with every application you send out, you need to make sure that your cover letter is actually helping you persuade your next employer to invite you in for an interview.

Many new professionals just simply Google "How to write a cover letter" and go with the first thing that pops up. These guides produce cover letters that are rigid and over-structured, and ultimately these cover letters do not help your potential employer understand exactly what you can do.

Do not submit a cover letter like this!

The number one mistake I see young professionals making when it comes to cover letters is forgetting this document is first and foremost a letter intended to be read by another human being. So, be interesting, inject personality, and compel the reader to keep reading. Those three elements are imperative to creating a cover letter that helps you get the interview.

If you are having a hard time writing your cover letter, try taking this slightly different approach:

Write down 3 to 5 main points you want to address in your cover letter in bullet point form. Then open up your phone's voice recording app, hit record, and take 30-60 seconds to talk about each one of the bullets. Once you're done, go back and transcribe what you said word for word.

This is the (very) rough draft of your new cover letter. Now you can edit, refine, and hone in your message since all of your thoughts are out of your head and onto the page.

Try this method now and see how it turns out!

The 5 points I want to address in my cover letter are:
1)

2)

3)

4)

5)

___

# Action #29: Create a professional portfolio

*"Show Your Work!"*
– Every 5th grade teacher

A visually compelling professional portfolio can have a greater impact on understanding your academic and professional accomplishments than words on a resume. Graphs, charts, pictures, and real-world examples of your work are an amazing way to continue to showcase your skills to your next employer.

Here are some examples of items you can include in your new professional portfolio:

1. Resume and cover letter
2. Visual representations of your skills and technical abilities
    a. Software
    b. Tools
    c. Technology
3. Examples of your previous professional and school work
    a. PDFs
    b. Graphs/Charts
    c. Pictures of projects
    d. Screenshots of websites or reports

4.  References and testimonials
    a.  Pictures and related testimonials from
        other professionals about the quality of
        your work

You can create your portfolio in PowerPoint or Keynote. It should be about 10 to 15 pages.

Bring this portfolio to your next interview and include it electronically every time you submit an application. It can be a unique and powerful way to help your next employer better understand what you are capable of, plus it helps separate you from the rest of the applicants.

My professional portfolio is # _______ pages, and includes:

1)

2)

3)

4)

5)

# Section 4: Making a Positive Impression on the Decision Maker

# Action #30: Develop your ability to tell memorable stories

*"Have a great story to tell ... and tell it well. No holds barred."*
*—Aishwarya Rai Bachchan, Bollywood Actress*

The worst interviews I have ever sat through all had something in common: they felt more like police interrogations than professional interviews. I can sum up each of these interviews like this: question, answer, question, answer. They were dull, forgettable, and  like pulling teeth!

Your interviews need to be positive conversations. The best way you can make sure this happens is by telling intriguing stories. Engage your audience with your words and not simply by replying with hypotheticals and what if's. Good stories have a beginning, a middle, and a conclusion—they have details, invoke emotion, and relate to the audience.

Whenever you tell a story in an interview, to your social circle, or in a conversation with another professional, make it a compelling one. Telling good stories builds social rapport, makes you memorable, and allows you to project the confidence needed to land that first career job after college.

___

Take a few minutes to fill out the questions below to flesh out your first good story:

1) Title of my story

2) Problem encountered

3) Names of the people involved

4) Solution/Final outcome

5) Lesson learned/Conclusion

Now, I want you to tell your story out loud and record it into your phone's voice recorder app.

- How long is your story:

- What are 3 things you did right when telling this story for the first time:

- What are 2 things you want to improve next time you tell this story:

Today _______________ (MM/DD/YY), I developed my _______________ (title) story to tell in my next interview.

# Action #31: Create a list of good professional stories to tell

You may think that since you're just graduating from college you don't have much life experience yet, but actually, that's not true. The bigger problem new professionals face is not a lack of good stories to tell, but the inability to remember those stories when they need them.

So many things happen to us on a daily basis, not to mention the information, messages, pictures, and status updates we are inundated with every time we open our phones. To combat this brain drain, you need to start actively documenting your good stories.

So, what is a good story? It is a story that has a good direct outcome or one where you were able to learn a valuable lesson. Too many people tend to only focus on the good outcomes, but having good stories with "bad" or unfavorable outcomes can be just as valuable. When you are telling stories in an interview, try to mix them up. If your stories  all have good, happy endings, you may look like you are lying or hiding something.

Real-time reflection is a major key to remembering and retelling the great stories that will help you connect with your next employer.

I recommend starting to send "Status Report" emails to yourself once a week to keep track of all the good stories that you can later use in interviews. Here are some rules you should follow to get the most out of this practice:

- The "Status Report" email subject should be formatted like this: *Status Report MM/DD/YYYY*
- Document the 3 memorable stories, lessons learned, successes, and failures from that week
- Stories should be written in quick 1-2 sentence summaries
- Take no more than 5 minutes to write this email

That's it! The next time you need to pull out a good story from your arsenal to answer an interview question, you now have real-time updates of important events in your professional life.

And since these are organized in your email, you can quickly search your inbox to recall stories. For example:

Search: "Status Report" + budget, "Status Report" + goal, "Status Report" + marketing project.

This Friday                                    (MM/DD/YY), I am going to write my first "Status Report" email.

The first story in the email will be about

# Action #32: Know how to effectively tell your next employer what your strengths are

*"Everyone knows that confidence is sexy, and it's knowing your assets, your strengths, and just playing those up."*
—Marisa Miller, American Model

Your next employer is going to hire you based on what you are good at.

You will be asked to identify these positive skills or characteristics in your next interview, and if you're not 100% confident about what they are and how to communicate them, you are going to lose out on a promising opportunity.

First off, you need to identify what your top strengths are. Write down your top 5 professional strengths here:

1)

2)

3)

4)

5)

Great!
Now, you can't just say you have these strengths and expect the manager to take your word for it. You need to be able to back up these strong statements with even stronger evidence.

So for every strength you listed above, I want you to write down a quick example of how that strength positively helped you on the job.

Example: *Persistence – closed the new online marketing contract with Sally's Dog Groomers on Main Street after 6 rejections.*

Strength 1)

Strength 2)

Strength 3)

Knowing these strengths and related stories will give you leverage when marketing yourself as a high-achieving professional to your next employer. They will need to know what your strengths are so they can utilize those strengths as much as possible, and so your manager can play to these strengths to help you do an even better job in your next position.

# Action #33: Identify your body language crutches

During your next professional interview, you may be filled with anxiety and struggle to keep your composure. It is in these high-stress moments that it becomes very easy to succumb to the bad habits you have developed over the years.

Whether you tap your feet, say "um" or "like," cross your arms, or are unable to maintain eye contact, everybody has body language crutches. If you can identify these physical or verbal tics and consciously be aware of them during your next interview, you can curb them so you're not distracting from the quality of the conversation that you're having with your next employer.

Below is a list of common body language crutches and how managers interpret them in interviews:

**Failure to make eye contact** - Threatened, Intimidated, Anxious, Lying

**Lack of voice quality** - Lying, Unprepared, Lack of Confidence

**Lack of a smile** - Unfriendly, Unwelcoming

**Bad posture** - Unkempt, Low Self Confidence

**Weak handshake** - Intimidated, Scared

**Crossing arms over chest** - Defensive, Blocking Out

Write down your top 3 body language crutches below:

1)

2)

3)

Not sure what your crutches are? Ask your friends or family, they can probably point out a few. Be hyper-aware next time you're in one of these high-stress situations to see how your body reacts. How does your adrenaline and anxiety affect the way you physically feel and act?

Now that you know what your crutches are, next time you go into an interview, in the upper right-hand corner of your notes write "Smile", or "Eye Contact", or "Slow Down." This will be a subtle reminder to curtail these impulses and keep yourself composed.

# Action #34: Understand why your employer may ask what your weaknesses are, and know how to answer the question

*"Build up your weaknesses until they become your strong points."*
*—Knute Rockne, Famed College Football Coach*

"What are your weaknesses?" may be one the most cliché, and feared, questions asked in an interview. Many people try to outsmart the question by providing an answer disguised as a weakness but that is really a strength, like: "I work too hard," "I care too much," or "I am a perfectionist."

When a manager hears these answers, they may automatically disqualify the candidate. Why? Because the candidate has misunderstood the purpose of the question itself.

The question is not presented to help you convince the decision maker not to hire you. It's actually quite the opposite: the employer wants to know if you are earnestly able to identify your own weaknesses and make proactive corrections.

If you can't do this for yourself, then how is your next
boss expected to give you feedback and expect positive
change?

Here are 3 keys to answering this question in your next
interview:

1. Be honest and state the weakness
2. Explain how this weakness hurt you in the past
3. Explain how you are improving this weakness

You need to be self-aware in order to take and act on
valid workplace criticism. Delivering an overused and
empty answer tells your next employer that you really
have no idea what your shortcomings are.

If you are having a hard time answering the question,
"What is my biggest weakness?" flip it on its head and
ask yourself, "What is the one thing I want to improve
about myself?"

Here, outline one of your biggest weaknesses:

1)      The weakness:


2)      Outline story about how this weakness has
        negatively affected you in the past:

# Action #35: Set up your battle station for your next interview

As you interview virtually and in-person, I encourage all my clients to ensure their "battle station" (either physically or digitally) is ready for each and every interview.

Here is what I recommend having at your station:

1.  Copies of your most updated resume. Share these with the interviewer(s) when the interview starts.
2.  The text from the job posting itself.
3.  Webpages with your and the interviewer's LinkedIn Profile pages.
4.  Your personal notes for the interview: outlines of stories you want to tell and questions you want to ask.

Why is all of this so important?

1) **You can use all this info as a safety net.** If you get a tricky question or simply have a brain fart, all you have to do is look at your documents and pick one bullet, job, or skillset to talk about to answer the question.

2) **Don't assume everyone is as prepared as you are.** Help the person interviewing you by coming prepared with your resume. They might not have your resume right in front of them.

3) **Your battle station will enhance the comprehension of the other people in the interview.** Ever wonder why teachers have elementary students read out loud as the rest of the class follows along? The more inputs we have of the same information, the more likely we are to remember it. Use this same concept to help your next boss remember you better by giving them something to read as you tell your stories.

4) **Leverage the info on the interviewers' LinkedIn profiles to make a personal connection.** Ask them about their own career, how they went from their previous job to their current one, or maybe even bring up a common connection. All this will help you be more memorable after the interview is over.

My personal interview battle station consists of:

Don't forget to download all the additional resources for this book.

Head to:

https://www.employedbygraduation.com/

Or scan the QR Code below:

# Section 5: Leveling Up your Job Search Strategy

# Action #36: Create your job search plan


*"Working hard and working smart sometimes can be two different things."*
*—Byron Dorgan, United States Senator*

Your success in this job search process (and in life) is rooted in small and constant actions, not large and infrequent ones. So, to ensure that you are ready to act once that amazing opportunity presents itself, and to guarantee that you are continuously progressing towards your goal of landing that career job before graduation, create a Job Search Plan for yourself.

A good plan will give you comprehensive daily, weekly, and monthly actions that keep you on task and maintain important momentum. A Job Search Plan eliminates your need to think and prioritize ... and procrastinate. All you will have to do is open up your plan on a daily basis and take action.

Here are a few actions you should have on your plan, but it is up to you to determine how frequently (daily, weekly, or monthly) you want to do them:

- Apply to 1 job
- Request to connect with 3 people on LinkedIn
- Have a conversation with a person of influence

- Check job sites
- Write and post a blog on LinkedIn
- Write a thank you card
- Practice a new interview question
- Attend a networking event
- Do 1 chapter from *Employed By Graduation*
- Schedule an coffee with a tenured professional
- Read a chapter of a non-fiction book related to desired career/industry
- Ask for help from 1 professional
- Make an introduction between 2 professionals you know
- Google yourself

Take some of the actions above (and include some of your own) in your new Job Search Plan below.

My daily tasks are:

My weekly tasks are:

My monthly tasks are:

# Action #37: Track your job search time

*"Time is beyond our control, and the clock keeps ticking regardless of how we lead our lives. Priority management is the answer to maximizing the time we have."*
*—John C. Maxwell, Leadership Expert and Best Selling Author*

Too many professionals—young and old—looking for new employment only focus on doing job search activities that may feel good and productive—checking job sites, going on LinkedIn, reading career related articles—but in reality, these actions are far from productive and can even end up being a complete detriment to the job search process.

The more "bad effort" you put into the job search process, the more bad results you will get out. If you continue down this path for too long, you will end up losing out on great opportunities, get stuck, and become unmotivated.

Here are the top 5 job search activities that could easily become unproductive if not kept in check:

1) Refreshing your preferred job board more than once a day; being the first to apply doesn't help your chances.
2) Spending too much time "perfecting" your resume for each application; your resume should be optimized so you only need 5-10 minutes of customization per application.
3) Crafting a totally new cover letter each time you apply; using a master cover letter template can help you optimize your time and energy in your search.
4) Falling down online research rabbit holes that feel productive but just waste time; ask yourself, is this research really helping me be the best candidate, or is it a "productive" distraction.
5) Multitasking! Make your job search your singular focus when you job search, without any external distractions.

This is why I HIGHLY recommend you start tracking all of your job search time and effort.

In the Downloadable Resources I've included a table to track your actions 15-minute increments. Now, after every 15 minutes you spend on your job search, input what you have been up to on the spreadsheet.

Using this tool diligently will help you keep tabs on your activities and ensure true productivity in your job search process.

Today ______________ (MM/DD/YY),
I worked for # ______ minutes on my job search.
I spent # ______ minutes doing productive work
and # ______ minutes doing busy work.

# Action #38: Actively track where and when you have applied

Being overly organized is going to help keep you on track—and keep you sane—during this job search process. With countless applications, websites, resumes, cover letters, and emails flying around, it can be all too easy to get turned around and confused while looking for your first career job.

Create a spreadsheet (or download the one from the Additional Resources) to help you keep everything in one place. Include the following columns: Job Title, Company, Job Posting URL, Date Applied, Date of Last Update. Every time you apply for a job, fill out all the information on your new Job Tracker Spreadsheet.

Using this tool diligently will help you stay on top of your job search. It will help you keep up with existing applications and, more importantly, make sure that you're following up with each application.

Been over a week since you submitted that application? Follow up!

Been over a month and still no word? Put that opportunity in the NO group.

Keeping track of applications can get really overwhelming and confusing if you're not tracking them accurately. You don't want to be caught off guard when you get a call or an email, and you don't want to let an opportunity fall through the cracks simply because you haven't been following up at the proper times.

Today _______________ (MM/DD/YY), I downloaded the Job Application Tracker spreadsheet.

I filled it out with the last # _______ jobs I applied for.

# Action #39: Stop playing the job lottery

You might hear that landing a new job is a numbers game: send out as many applications as possible and you will land an interview eventually. But this is a friendly reminder that your success is not purely dependent on luck or chance!

Too many new graduates play this "job lottery" and then struggle when they aren't called back for interviews. And this is where burnout happens.

When we burn out in the job search, we tend to a) procrastinate (until it's too late) or b) settle for a job well below our capabilities simply to escape the process. So don't let this be you!

Today, shift your approach to focus on quality and not simply quantity with your applications. Take a little more time to get specific on what's important to you in your new role. So, instead of applying to 10 jobs you are qualified to do, prioritize the top 5 that excite you, can lead to more career growth, or are at companies whose values resonate with you.

Focusing your efforts will give you more time to customize your application, conduct personalized outreach, and diligently follow up. It is important to avoid any quick or easy apply button you see.

This concentrated application strategy can make a big difference in getting you more interviews, keeping you excited about the process, and ensuring you can choose where you want to start your career and not just settle for whatever comes first.

The last job I played the "job lottery" on was:

The next job I am going to take my time and strategically apply for is:

# Action #40: Apply to 1 job today

The old adage is true: a bird in the hand is worth 2 in the bush. Which is why employers would rather get you on board before you graduate, knowing you'll be ready to go once you cross the stage. Do not wait until after graduation to start applying for jobs!

Starting now, just like the title of this book implies, greatly increases your chances of getting an amazing job versus waiting until you, and everyone else, has crossed the stage. In 2025, over 5 million new college graduates will enter the workforce[4]. And if you wait, they WILL become your competition.

Even if you have big plans after graduation—backpacking across Europe, volunteering in a third-world country, or simply just taking a well-deserved breather—do not wait! Many employers are willing to accommodate you and your plans, especially if you get everything finalized well in advance.

Today _______________ (MM/DD/YY), I applied for _______________ (job), at _______________ (company).

---

[4] Hanson, Melanie, "College Graduation Statistics (updated March 5, 2024),", EducationData.org, https://educationdata.org/number-of-college-graduates.

# Action #41: Ask for help with one thing

*"The most important thing I think we need to remember is that we're a work in progress. Do not be ashamed or afraid to ask for help."*
*—Carnie Wilson, American Singer*

As is true in life, not every action in this book is something you can complete solely on your own. And since you are reading this book, I have to assume that you are already adept at understanding your need for help and actively pursuing it.

Write down the top action in this book that you have been putting off because you don't know how to complete it:

Action:

Now, jot down 3 people that could help you take action:

1)

2)

3)

# Action #42: Now, ask for help, better

The #1 request I get in my inbox is "Can you help me find a job?" The short answer is yes, but I rarely respond to these types of requests.

Why? They lack any important information, like a desired job title, specific company, or even something as simple as attaching a resume.

This tells me that this person wants me to do all the heavy lifting for them. And I, like all professionals, am a busy person. My lack of response does not mean that I don't have good intentions and like to blatantly ignore people. Instead it means I have a busy work and home life and I guard the precious free time I do have. I do not want to fill that time trying to chase down someone asking for my help.

Simply asking for help doesn't mean you're going to get it. You need to make sure that you're asking for help in a specific way that actually gets you the assistance you need.

Provide all necessary information and items to limit back-and-forth and ensure that your request is granted.

Include things like your resume, cover letter, LinkedIn profile URL, professional portfolio, or link to the job opportunity. The more information you can provide, the easier it will be to execute in your favor.

Your request needs to be obvious and your call to action should be clear. What is the one thing you need that person to do for you? Make sure you state that at the end of the email.

Lastly, give a deadline. This allows the professional to mentally earmark the steps needed to fulfill your request in the given timeframe.

Your goal is to eliminate as much work on the other person's end and ensure your favor is as turnkey as possible, so it gets done correctly and quickly.

Here is an email script you can steal:

*"Hi Erin,*
*In preparation for graduation and embarking on my first career job search, I have been reading this great book, Employed By Graduation. I have been making great progress, and would be really appreciative if you could help me with a recommendation on LinkedIn.*

*I wanted to reach out and see if you could help me complete it this week by writing out 3-4 sentences of our time working together at the law firm and how I was able to help you with that new filing system.*

*I would really appreciate your assistance, hopefully it won't take you more than 5 minutes. I will check back Friday to see if you have any questions.*

*Thanks!"*

# Action #43: Find one way to gain some additional professional experience

Today, simply having that college degree isn't going to be enough of a differentiator to help you land your first career job. A good mix of professional, leadership, and volunteer experience will put you head and shoulders above your competition.

So go out now and gain even a little bit of additional professional experience.

Explore a temporary job, internships, externships, one-off projects, volunteer opportunities, or a leadership role in an organization. Making that one last push to gain more experience or skills before you cross the stage could be the difference between landing that first full-time job quick or floating around, unemployed.

This additional opportunity will add to the foundation of professional experience you already have, while giving you further opportunities to build your network.

Today _______________________ (MM/DD/YY),
Applied to the _______________ internship/job.
Asked my boss to take on the ________ project.
Emailed about volunteering at _______________

# Action #44: Ask one professional about an unadvertised job opportunity

Last year, 60% of all available job opportunities were never advertised to the general public[5]. Of the approximately 7.4 million jobs available, over 4.4 million of them never ended up on a company's career page or on a job site like Indeed or LinkedIn. The only way to learn about these hidden opportunities was by knowing a professional who was aware they existed. Companies keep these jobs "hidden" so they can attract only the highest quality applicants, usually through personal referrals from their current employees.

Tap into this secret job market! Contact one professional in your network and ask them directly if there are any jobs that are in the pipeline, but have not been posted to the public yet, that you might qualify for.

If they respond yes, see if that professional can send you the job description and then send over your resume and cover letter (tailored to the job).

---

[5]  Harden, Paige, "How to Land a Job by Networking," *The Washington Post*, May 23, 2016, https://jobs.washingtonpost.com/article/how-to-land-a-job-by-networking/.

If there is nothing currently available in their company, thank them, send over your professional documents, and ask them if they would keep you in mind when the next opportunity comes up.

Keep track of who you are sending these requests to and touch base with them every other month to see if anything new has popped up on their internal job boards.

Name of professional:


Date of email:

# Action #45: Google yourself

Your next employer is going to Google you, there's no way around it. So what are they going to find when they do? Do you know what Google is showing your next employer when they search for you?

Take 30 seconds right now to type  your first and last name into Google and write down the top 5 results:

1)

2)

3)

4)

5)

Of those results, how many are giving your next employer a positive impression about you? How many give them a negative one? What about a neutral impression?

To actively create a positive, professional online personal brand: update your LinkedIn profile, create a portfolio website, or privatize your social media account. This will help you separate yourself from other applicants who have no online presence, or who have an unsavory, unprofessional one.

Conduct this "vanity" search once per month to keep on top of what information is popping up when someone looks for you on Google.

The next time I will do this search is ___________ (MM/DD/YY).

# Action #46: Set up your own website

Your next employer is going to Google you. And what they find can either help or hurt your candidacy, so be proactive in what they are going to find and easily separate yourself from others by setting up your own website.

Unlike in the early days of the internet, you don't need a degree in computer science to set up and launch your own website. With services like Wix.com, About.me, and Squarespace, you can quickly and easily set up an informative and attractive personal site.

Here is a checklist of items you should feature on your website:

- Name, phone number, email address, LinkedIn profile link

- PDF version of your resume

- Examples of prior relevant work (i.e. reports, presentations, screenshots of projects)

- Photos of you doing your job or in a professional setting

- Testimonials from other professionals about your work

Take your online personal brand to the next level by buying your own vanity URL (firstnamelastname.com), and setting up a forward to your personal website. Feature this URL on your resume, LinkedIn profile, and in your email signature.

Make your website as important as your resume, cover letter, or LinkedIn profile when marketing yourself during your job search.

Today                         (MM/DD/YY), I created my website:                         (URL).

# Action #47: Go to your next campus career fair

On average today, job openings receive over 250 applications[6]. And with a large majority of candidates simply submitting their resume and moving on, you have the opportunity to set yourself apart by putting a face to the name on your resume.

The most opportune time to do this is during your campus' next career fair or corporate visit. While these events can be overcrowded with students seeking jobs, here are a few things you can do before, during, and after the next career fair you attend to help you stand out from the crowd:

- **Before the fair**: Research the companies that will be at the career fair. Identify your top 10 organizations and go on their websites to see if they have any current openings that you are interested in. Be professionally dressed and bring extra resumes, business cards, and your professional portfolio. Ideally all of your documents (including your portfolio) should be left with the manager or recruiter at the

---

[6] Chamberlain, Andrew, *Glassdoor's Job and Hiring Trends for 2020*, https://www.glassdoor.com/research/app/uploads/sites/2/2019/11/Job_Hiring_Trends_2020-FINAL-1-1.pdf

company's booth, so bring a good number of each.

- **During the fair**: Make a professional and lasting impression when you meet these professionals face-to-face. Mention the job opportunities you found online and tell them why you have prioritized their company over others. Lastly, hand over your documents and get a business card from them.

- **After the fair**: Follow up with the companies and professionals you talked with a couple of days after the fair to stay on their radar. Connect with the people you met on LinkedIn. When you do finally apply to a position at their company, reach out to them directly so they can pick you out of the pile of countless other faceless names they've received as applicants.

My next campus career fair is      (MM/DD/YY). I will put it on my calendar now.

# Action #48: Get business cards made

You don't need a fancy corporate job title to have business cards—they prove extremely valuable in social and professional networking situations, and you can get them made online for next to nothing. The act of exchanging information has become a lot less formal since we all started carrying smartphones, and great looking professional business cards are an amazing way to make a memorable parting impression. It shows that you're prepared, professional, and, again, it's a positive differentiator from your peers in similar situations.

On your new business cards put the following information:

First and last name
Phone number
Email address
LinkedIn profile or personal URL
3-5 core professional competencies

Your business card may read something like this:

John Student
(619) 213-1234
johnstudent@gmail.com
johnstudent.net
Digital Marketing, Search Engine Optimization, Social
Media Marketing

Once you get your business cards made, keep them on
you at all times! You never know the next time you
might need them.

Today                          (MM/DD/YY),
I created and ordered #          business cards
from

# Action #49: Start using social proof in your job search

The old adage is still true: It isn't what you know, but WHO you know. And with sites like LinkedIn, Instagram, and Facebook, leveraging your network in the search for your first career job is necessary, especially when the average job opening receives over 250 applications. Incorporating elements of social proof into your job search can make a world of difference.

So what is social proof? We see it most often in traditional advertising: testimonials, reviews, and recommendations. Instead of having the product tout its features, social proof allows customers to talk about its benefits—think celebrity endorsements, "actual customers," or online reviews. Research has proven that this kind of communication is strongest when trying to persuade someone to make a decision. And you should be using it as you look for jobs.

Your strongest form of social proof are your professional references.

Contact at least 3 career professionals you know who can deliver an honest and powerful recommendation for you. Do your best to avoid relatives, professors, or peers—their words don't carry as much weight as a person who has a purely professional relationship with you.

Professional 1:

Professional 2:

Professional 3:

Bonus Tip: Have these professionals leave you a Recommendation on your LinkedIn profile as well. Use those same recommendations in your professional portfolio.

Today                              (MM/DD/YY), I asked 3 professionals to be my references.

# BONUS Action #50: Go above and beyond expectations

There is going to be a lot of competition out there as you graduate from college and try to land your first career job. And with the sheer number of applicants, you need to be actively separating yourself from the pack.

Ultimately, your goal as a job applicant is to positively differentiate yourself from everyone else. Too many of your peers will try to play it safe and be conservative when it comes to how they approach the application processes, making them indistinguishable from one another and lumped into the big pile of "average."

Many of the actions in this book have helped you go above and beyond: submitting a great cover letter, presenting a professional portfolio, or writing a thank you letter.

Here are a few more to try:
- Directly call the company to let them know you've applied or to check up on your application
- Connect with HR or the hiring manager on LinkedIn
- Get a formal introduction over email by someone you already know at the company

So, at every single point of this job search process, you need to be taking an action that will go above and beyond the expectations for a regular applicant.

Write down the last three jobs you applied for and come up with 3 ways you can stand out from the rest of the applicants by doing something positively unexpected:

Job:
Above and Beyond Action:

Job:
Above and Beyond Action:


Job:
Above and Beyond Action:


Today                              (MM/DD/YY), I went above and beyond on 3 of my applications.

Don't forget to download all the additional resources for this book.

Head to:

**https://www.employedbygraduation.com/**

Or scan the QR Code below:

# Conclusion

So there you have it, 50-plus actions you can take NOW to get you that much closer to landing your first career job right out of college!

I want to thank you for taking the time to read this book and to put in the effort. I'm sure it was not all easy: you had to push yourself, leave your comfort zone, and think long and hard. But I promise you all that work is worth it!

By doing this hard work now, you are going to enable yourself to start off your career on a great foot and avoid needing to make more painful choices down the road. I work with countless professionals in the middle of their careers who wake up and realize their career has been built on happenstance, accident, or dumb luck. They all wish they had done this important work way earlier so they could have avoided all the headache and heartache, so they could have done more of the work they truly love, and so they could have been able to strike a healthy work/life balance.

But now that you've finished reading the book, it's time for the rubber to hit the road and for you to continue to take meaningful action.

The key to success in this process is consistent, small actions. Continue to take small steps regularly to achieve that big, amazing goal.

I would love to hear from you about your successes in this process, learn what you may be struggling with, or how the next edition of this book could be improved for future  college graduates.

Lastly, if you feel like this book added value to your job search process, share it with someone who you know is struggling—a friend who has changed majors a few times, a classmate who has expressed their anxiety about post-college life, or an old roommate who may just stick with that hourly job instead of leveling up their career to do the kind of work they are made to do.

Succeeding in your post-college job search (and life!) is all about starting NOW!

# About The Author

Kolby Goodman is the founder of the personal consulting and training firm, The Job Huntr, and has been successfully providing programs in career advancement and job satisfaction since 2013.

His clients have landed amazing jobs at the nation's top companies, including Apple, Google, Amazon, Tesla, Workday, Salesforce, Qualcomm, Intuit, and ResMed among others. He's also partnered with Panasonic, Starwood Hospitality Group, American Association of Pharmaceutical Scientists, several universities and schools, national professional organizations and nonprofits to provide tailored workshops.

He is also proud to partner with San Diego State University, University of California, San Diego, University of San Diego, and Notre Dame University.

Kolby is a proud San Diego State University Aztec, devoted husband to Allison, and considers being a dad to his two boys his greatest privilege.

kolby@thejobhuntr.com
https://www.linkedin.com/in/kolbygoodman/